My Book of Indian Tales
of wit & humour

The Monkey and the Crocodile

Long ago, there was a cheerful monkey who lived on a tree near the sea. This tree bore delicious fruits which the monkey ate every day. One day, a crocodile came ashore and started resting under this tree. The monkey had no friends, so he wished to befriend him. He said, "This tree is my home. Since you are my guest, you must have these fruits."

The crocodile took the fruits, which the monkey gave him.

Soon, they became good friends. Once, the crocodile wanted to take some fruits for his wife. Delighted, the monkey gave them to him. When the crocodile came home, his wife heard his story and greedily ate the fruits. She said, "If these fruits are so delicious, imagine how much tastier the monkey will be who eats these fruits. Bring the monkey's heart for me."

The crocodile was shocked. He replied, "The monkey is my good friend. How can I betray him?" But his wife insisted.

The poor crocodile had no choice but to carry out his wife's wishes. As he could not ask his friend for his heart, he made a plan. He went to the monkey, who was waiting for him, and said, "My wife has invited you for dinner. She wants to meet you."

The monkey was happy when he heard this. He accepted the invitation at once. As the monkey couldn't swim, the crocodile carried him on his back. So they set off on the journey. Soon they entered the deep sea.

Meanwhile, the crocodile decided to kill the monkey here.

The monkey was frightened on seeing so much water. So, he asked the crocodile to go slowly.

The crocodile decided to reveal everything to his friend as he felt the monkey was helpless now and could not possibly do anything to save himself. So the foolish crocodile began, "My wife wishes to eat your heart. She says that since you eat such delicious fruits all the time, you must have a wonderfully delicious heart."

The monkey was greatly shocked when he heard this. He soon overcame his initial fright and with great presence of mind, he replied, "Oh! It would be the greatest honour to give my heart to your dear wife. But you see I keep my heart safely hidden inside the tree. To fulfil her wishes, I must go back to get my heart. If you will take me back to the tree, I will get it as fast as possible."

The crocodile agreed to his request and they went back to the tree. Then, the frightened monkey jumped back on to the tree. The crocodile then asked him to hurry up.

But the monkey laughed and scolded him. "You cheat! I tricked you into saving my life. Do you think one's heart can be kept in a tree? Go away and never come back."

The crocodile felt guilty and went home, his head hung down in shame.

The Cat, the Partridge and the Hare

Once, there lived a partridge in a safe, warm hollow under a tree in a forest. Unfortunately, he had no proper source of food and often went hungry. So, he decided to go out to the fields and search for food. Having found plenty of food there, he did not return for many days.

While the partridge was away, a hare was passing through the forest. Soon, he came upon the partridge's home and liked it very much. He decided to live there. When the partridge returned fatter and healthier, he wanted his old home back.

The hare refused to leave his new home but the stubborn partridge would not listen either. Soon, a big fight broke out between them. Then, the two decided to approach the cat with their problem. Now, the cat was a hypocrite. He pretended to be a priest to earn his livelihood. The cat wished to eat the partridge and the hare. He was delighted when he saw them coming towards him.

"My friends," cried the cat, "please do not fight. I will help solve your problem."

The partridge and the hare began telling the cat their problem. As they stood far away, the cat said, "I can't hear you properly. Come nearer and tell me your story. Don't be afraid. I won't harm you."

So they went near him. Then the cat caught them both, killed them and had an enjoyable meal.

Gold's Gloom

There once lived a hermit named Sadhu. Every day he would go out to beg for food. His alms-bowl would always be filled with delicious eatables which people would offer him. He would eat his fill and hang the alms-bowl, with the leftover food, on the wall for his servant.

Now, a mouse called Chuha lived in the hermit's hut. Chuha used to nibble away at the food that the hermit hung up from the peg. He would even call his friends to share the meal.

One day, the hermit caught the mouse eating the food. So, he started hanging the food even higher. But that did not help as the mouse always managed to reach it. Once, Sadhu was visited by his friend, a fellow hermit. His friend started narrating a story. But Sadhu was more worried about the mouse eating the food. He kept hitting the alms-bowl with a bamboo stick. Seeing his companion's lack of interest in the story, the hermit became quite angry.

"Since you are not interested in my story at all, I shall leave. You have become very proud, just because you own a hut. This pride has earned you a place in hell!" Sadhu's friend shouted.

Sadhu was terrified when he heard this. He explained that his attention was on the alms-bowl because a mouse would eat all the leftover food. So, he had to hit the food bowl to frighten away the mouse.

"Oh! Is that so? Then we should think of a way of getting rid of this mouse," said the hermit.

"He often brings an army of mice with him," said Sadhu.

"Do you have any digging tools?" asked the hermit.

"Yes," said Sadhu and brought out a pickaxe. "But why do you want this?"

"I think that the mouse has wealth hidden in his hole. It is the smell of wealth that makes him and his companions so bold that they eat your food without the fear of getting caught.

We should get up early in the morning and follow their footprints while the floor is still dusty and dirty with them," said the hermit. Sadhu agreed with his friend's plan at once.

Now, it so happened that Chuha was listening to their conversation. He got scared and alerted the other mice. All of them left the house that same night.

On their way out, disaster struck. A cat pounced on them. Many mice were killed and many others were wounded. Those who survived, scolded Chuha for his decision to leave the hermit's hut. They decided to return to the hut. As they were going back to the hut, they left behind a trail of blood.

Chuha, however, did not go in with them.

The next morning, Sadhu saw the trail of blood and followed it. When he finally reached the mouse-hole, he began digging with a pickaxe. As he dug, he came across a hoard of gold coins. He took the entire hoard away.

Later, Chuha came back to the hole. He got a big shock when he realised that all his coins were gone.

In this unhappy state, Chuha decided to get his treasure back. So one night, he went and started gnawing at the bag in which the treasure was kept. Unfortunately his plan did not work. At that moment, Sadhu woke up and started hitting Chuha with a bamboo stick. But Chuha was too quick for him. He soon managed to flee the hermit's house and never returned to the house again. Thus, Sadhu successfully got rid of the mouse that kept eating up all his food.

Ramu – the Weaver

Once upon a time, in a small city, there lived a weaver called Ramu. He spent hours making beautiful garments, which were fit for a prince's wardrobe. But despite all his hard work, he was not able to earn enough money. He saw other weavers around him who weaved coarse cloth and yet managed to earn quite a lot of money.

One day, he told his wife, "I don't seem to be earning enough in this city. I am going to go elsewhere to earn a living. I will become rich and then return home."

His wife tried to dissuade him but he would not listen to her pleas. He packed up his belongings and went to another city. Ramu stayed there for three years and earned three hundred gold coins. After three years, he decided to return home.

On his way back, he had to cross a forest. As the sun was about to set, the weaver decided to rest in the forest for the night. He selected a stout banyan tree, hid his bag of gold coins in a hole in the tree and slept there.

At midnight, some noises woke him up from his sleep. He saw two human-like figures standing near him, with bloodshot eyes, who were arguing and abusing each other.

One of them was saying, "Shyam, for all these years, you prevented Ramu from earning a lot of money and now, you have given him three hundred gold coins!"

So Shyam explained to Laxman, the other man, that he had been forced to reward Ramu for his hard work. He said, "If you wish, you can take it away."

Upon hearing this, Ramu looked for his money, but it was gone. Losing his hard earned money upset him. So, he decided to go back to the city to earn some more money.

Thus, he earned five hundred gold coins in a single year. He left for home, taking a different route this time.

But at sunset, he reached the same banyan tree and went to sleep there.

At midnight, he woke up hearing the same voices arguing fiercely once again. Laxman was asking Shyam why Ramu was given those five hundred gold coins.

Shyam said, "I must reward the enterprising." Then, Ramu quickly checked his bag on hearing this exchange and found it empty again. He got very upset and decided to end his life. Just then, a voice said, "I am He who takes your money yet gives you just enough for food and clothes. If you need anything, ask me." When Ramu wished for wealth, he was asked why he wanted so much more than he really needed.

"I desire wealth because anyone who is rich becomes famous," said Ramu.

"Granted, but first go back to the city where two brothers, Gopal and Bhola live. Observe them and decide whether you need the money," said the voice.

He returned to the city and found Gopal's house. Grudgingly, Ramu was allowed to stay there. He wasn't offered dinner and nobody spoke to him either.

Then, Ramu went to Bhola's house. Here, he was greeted warmly. A feast was laid out for him and he was even given new garments. When he saw Bhola's hospitality, he realised that though Gopal had a lot of money, he was unkind and did not treat Ramu well. Whereas Bhola who had little money, was quite generous.

So, he happily returned home and prayed to God to make him a good person who uses his money wisely.

The Little Mice and the Big Elephants

Once, an earthquake struck a poor village. All the villagers abandoned it and went away. Soon, mice began to inhabit the ruins and it became a mice colony. This village was situated near a lake. A herd of elephants would go there daily to drink water. As they passed by the village, hundreds of mice would get hurt as the elephants would trample them.

Day by day, the problem grew worse.

Then, the king mouse decided to meet the king elephant. When he met the elephant, he said, "Sir, we stay in the village near the lake. Each time your herd enters the village, my mice get hurt. Please change your route. If you help us now, I promise you that we will help you whenever you need us."

Then the king elephant remarked, laughing, "You mice are too small to help us. But we will change our route so that no harm befalls you." The king mouse thanked him and returned home.

One day, a band of hunters came to that place and trapped some elephants in strong nets. The poor animals were unable to free themselves.

Then, the king elephant remembered the promise of the king mouse – that he would help the elephants in their hour of need. He realised that the tiny mice could bite through the nets and free his herd.

He called one of his subjects, who was not caught in the trap. He asked the messenger to go tell the king mouse what had happened and seek his immediate help.

On hearing about the incident, the king mouse led his mice to the exact spot where the elephants were trapped. They soon found the elephants. Then, the king mouse asked his subjects to free their friends. The mice soon freed the elephants. The elephants were filled with gratitude and thereafter, the mice and the elephants lived peacefully together.

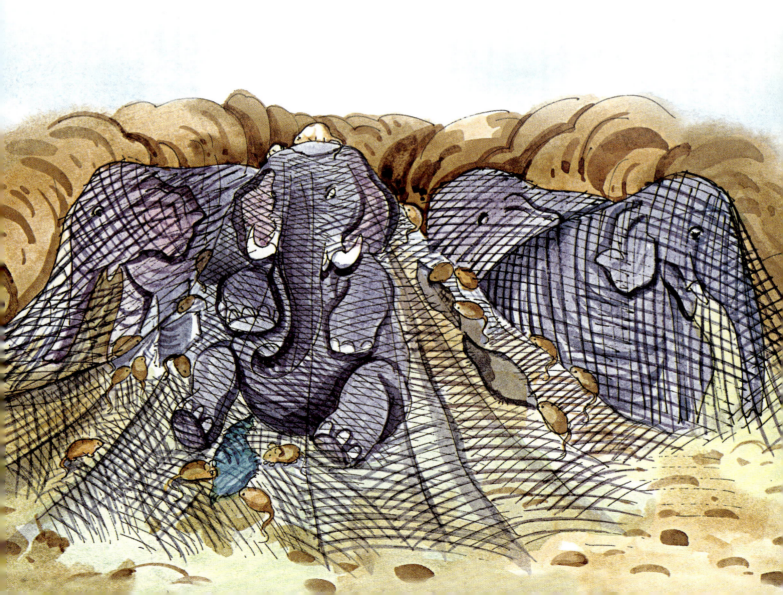

The Stork and the Crab

Once upon a time, a lazy stork lived near the edge of a pond. He wished to get his supply of fish without working too hard. So, he devised a cunning plan. One day, he went to the pond, looking sad and morose. In the same pond, there lived a wise and kind crab. He would help the fish there whenever they needed him. While the stork sat there, the crab too came to the same place.

When he saw the unhappy stork, the crab asked, "Pray, brother, what is the matter?"

The stork replied, "The pond is my only source of fish. But alas, I heard a few fishermen say that they will be catching all the fish in the pond in a week."

The fish grew worried when they heard the news.

Then, the cunning stork said, "I know a safer place. It's a bit far from here. If you wish, I will carry you to that pond."

All the creatures in the pond agreed.

The stork, however, said that he would need to rest between these trips as he was getting quite old. Also, he could carry only one fish at a time.

So each time, the stork would take a fish in his beak. But instead of going to the pond, he took it to a large rock and there, he would eat it. Then he would rest till the next trip.

The stork, thus, got his food regularly and soon became plump and healthy. Meanwhile, the crab became suspicious. So, he asked to be taken next. The greedy stork agreed.

As they walked, the crab asked, "Where is the pond?"

The stork felt that the crab was helpless and could not do anything now. He said, "You foolish crab. There is no pond nearby.

I did this so I could get my daily food. Now, you too will die."

Angered by his treachery, the crab dug his claws into the stork's neck. He bit off his head and the stork died. The crab then returned to his friends in the pond, and told them the whole story. The fish praised his courage and effort and thanked him for saving their lives.

The Sparrow and the Elephant

Once there lived a sparrow and her husband on a banyan tree. The sparrow had laid her eggs in her nest there.

One afternoon, an angry elephant shook the banyan tree and the nest fell down. All the sparrow's eggs were crushed. The female sparrow wept bitterly at the loss of her eggs.

The woodpecker asked her why she was crying. She replied weeping, "The elephant has killed all my children. That wicked creature must die."

The woodpecker consoled her and promised to help her kill the wicked elephant.

Both went to seek the fly's help. The woodpecker said, "Dear fly, this is my friend whose eggs were crushed by the wild elephant. Please help her."

The fly then said, "My friend, the frog will help us. Let us visit him."

So they went to the frog and told her their whole story.

The frog said, "I have an idea. Fly, you must go to the elephant and hum a tune in his ears. When he shuts his eyes, the woodpecker will pluck his eyes out and blind him.

When he is thirsty, he will want water. Then, I will go to a marshy area and start croaking. Thinking that there is water nearby, the elephant will come there and sink into the marshy land."

The next day, all three went about their plan. The elephant fell into the trap and he was killed as he sank in the marshy area, after being blinded by the woodpecker. Thus, the sparrow took her revenge on the elephant.

The Blue Jackal

In a dense forest, bordering a village, lived a sly jackal. Once, he entered the village, when some dogs started chasing him. So, he hid inside a house. There, he fell into a tub of blue dye.

Once the dogs stopped barking, the jackal came out. A big mirror lay nearby. On seeing himself in it, he was shocked and ran off into the forest. When the jackal reached the forest, no one recognised him. Instead, they ran away in fear.

But the clever jackal said to them, "Don't go away. I am God's special creation. The animals in this jungle had no ruler. So, he made me your king."

The animals accepted him as their king. The jackal made the lion his chief minister, the tiger his chamberlain and the wolf his gatekeeper. He then threw out all the jackals from his kingdom as he was afraid that they would recognise him.

The animals would hunt for food and bring it to the jackal, who would take his share and give the remaining to his subjects.

One day, the jackal was at court. A herd of jackals was passing by and started howling. Then, the blue jackal's natural instinct made him howl along with them. At once, the other animals knew that the blue jackal had fooled them. Enraged, they caught the jackal and killed him.

Unity is Strength

In a forest, stood a huge banyan tree. A crow named Kauwa lived here. Once, he saw a hunter coming towards the tree.

The hunter was followed by dogs, and he carried a snare and a club in his hands. Kauwa got scared and thought, 'I'm sure he wants to kill me.'

Kauwa watched with bated breath to see what the hunter would do.

The hunter selected a spot, spread his net there, scattered some grains and hid in the bushes.

Meanwhile, Kauwa had warned the other birds about the hunter. So none of them came to feed.

After some time, the dove-king called Kabutar came there with hundreds of other doves. They saw the grains. In spite of Kauwa's warning, they flew down to eat. And they all got caught in the trap.

The hunter was very happy with his catch. The dove-king and his mates were in a helpless state. Then, Kabutar realised he had to free them. He decided to encourage them.

He told them, "We should fly together and carry the net away. We need to be united because death befalls those who are not."

"How is that?" asked the doves.

So Kabutar told them the story of the bharunda birds.

"These birds had one belly and two necks. One day, one of them went in search of food. The first neck found some nectar. The second neck asked the first neck to give it some, but it refused. So, the second neck got angry and ate some poison. Since they shared the same belly, both of them died. That is why it is said, 'Unity is strength'."

The doves were inspired by the story. And, together, they carried the net away.

The hunter was very surprised when he saw the doves carrying the net away. He decided to follow the birds. Even Kauwa followed them. The hunter chased them for some time, but seeing the futility of it, he gave up.

Kabutar directed the doves in the north-easterly direction. There his friend, a mouse called Chuha, lived.

He was confident that Chuha would help them by gnawing at the ropes.

On reaching the mouse-hole, Kabutar asked him to bite through the net.

So Chuha began with gnawing Kabutar's bonds. But Kabutar stopped him and said, "Please start with my followers."

"How can I possibly do that? Servants follow the master. I should cut your bonds first and then those of your followers," said Chuha.

"No, my friend," said Kabutar, "all these doves left their flocks for me. They helped me and I must do the same."

Chuha understood Kabutar's feelings and praised him. "Yes, of course," said Chuha, gazing admiringly at the dove-king. "I was just trying to test you. I will respect your wishes and begin by freeing them first."

So the mouse set about his task. He started to nibble away at the net and bit by bit, he tore through it. Soon, all the birds were freed, including Kabutar. All the doves were overjoyed on being set free. They praised the dove-king's wisdom and generosity. He had just taught them that being united and keeping others needs above one's own brings happiness to all.

Kabutar and the other birds thanked Chuha and they all flew back home, enjoying and appreciating their freedom once more. On the way back home, a young dove said, "Our leader may be old but he is wise. It is because of him that we were saved."

"No, our unity saved us," said Kabutar.

The Crow and the Black Snake

Once upon a time, there lived a crow with his wife on a big banyan tree. In the same tree, lived a black snake, who would eat up all the crow's young ones, as soon as they were born.

The crow and his wife were very unhappy, but the crow refused to leave the banyan tree.

Finally, the crow's wife begged her husband to leave the tree. Since all her children had been eaten up by the snake, she did not wish to live on the same tree.

"We have lived all our lives on this tree. We cannot leave it. Be patient. I will think of a plan to get rid of the snake," said the crow.

"But," said his wife, "how will you kill this poisonous snake?"

"My friends will help me kill him," said the crow. The crow then went to his friend, the jackal. He told him the whole story of how the snake had eaten up all his children and asked for his help.

The jackal reassured the crow that a cruel snake like that would surely have to die. He came up with a clever, ingenuous plan to get them rid of the snake. He asked the crow to get hold of the king's gold chain.

Then, he advised the crow to leave the chain near the snake so that the snake would be killed when the chain was found by the king's men.

So, the crow and his wife set off in search of a gold necklace. They searched everywhere and soon came to a lake. The crow's wife soon spotted some women of the king's court playing in the water. They had removed their ornaments and placed them on the bank of the river. At once, she saw a gold chain among the ornaments lying on the ground.

Quick as lightning, the wife flew down to the river bank, picked up a gold chain and flew back to the tree where she lived. Then, she dropped the chain in the snake's hole and waited at a distance to see what would happen.

Now, the attendants had seen the crow flying away with the chain. So they followed her and saw her dropping the chain into a hole in the banyan tree. The attendants returned to the lake where the king's men had come back after their hunting trip. They informed the soldiers that a gold chain had been stolen and it was now lying in a small hole in a banyan tree where a fierce-looking black snake lived. The attendants directed the king's men towards the tree.

When the king's men reached the hole, they saw the black snake in it. At once, they killed it with their spears, took the chain and went away. Thus, the crows got rid of the cruel black snake which had tormented them for so long.

Thereafter, the crow and his wife continued to live in peace on the banyan tree.

The Sensible Enemy

Once upon a time, there lived a prince who had two very close friends. One of them was a merchant's son and the other was the son of a scholar. Every day, they would spend their time playing games or relaxing in parks and gardens.

The king wished that his son would develop an interest in royal pastimes. But the prince refused to learn the art of archery, elephant riding or hunting. The prince showed his dislike for these activities quite openly, much to the dismay of the king. The king soon got tired of the prince's stubborn behaviour and scolded him severely. He told him that he could not be a good king, as he showed no interest in royal pursuits. This was a huge blow to his self esteem.

The prince, unhappy with his father's remarks, went and told his friends what his father had said. His friends nodded.

"Our fathers also scold us for not showing interest in their professions," said his friends.

The prince thought for a while and then said, "I have a plan. Let us go somewhere and earn some money."

The other friends agreed with him, but they did not know where to go or how they could possibly earn a lot of money in a short time.

At last, the merchant's son said, "Let us go to the Climbing Mountain where we may find precious gems." The boys liked the idea and set out for the Climbing Mountain.

Soon enough, they reached the mountain. They travelled through the rough terrain all the while searching for treasure. Luck was in their favour and each of them found a priceless gem. Now, they were faced with another problem – the problem of guarding the jewels and taking them back safely to their city.

The son of the scholar said, "I have a plan. We should swallow the gems and carry them back in our stomachs. Then, they will be completely safe."

The others agreed and along with their food, they swallowed the gems. They decided to continue their journey. Meanwhile, a man hiding behind the bushes, overheard them and saw them swallowing the gems. He was filled with greed and wished to possess the gems.

He thought, 'I have also been searching for gems for so many days but found none at all. So, I will travel with them and when they go off to sleep, I will cut their stomachs open and take all the three gems.'

With this plan in mind, he approached them and said, "Good friends, I cannot go through the forest all alone. Please allow me to join you and travel with you." The three friends agreed to the man's request and resumed their journey.

In the middle of the rugged forest was a small village. As the travellers passed through the outskirts of the village, an old bird in a cage began to sing. Now, this was no ordinary bird.

He was the village chief's pet. The chief understood the meaning of everything the bird said. He erupted in joy and told his men, "Listen, the bird says there are precious gems with the travellers on the jungle trail. Stop them and bring them here! Search them thoroughly."

So, the villagers went and brought them before the chief. The chief had them searched carefully but found nothing on them. So, he set them free to continue their journey.

But, the bird continued singing the same song. So, the travellers were brought back, searched and freed once more. The bird, however, did not stop singing, so the chief called them back again and said, "I know this bird never tells a lie. He says that you are carrying some gems with you. Where are they?"

"If we have gems with us, how is it that you could not find them, in spite of searching twice?" said one of them.

"If the bird repeatedly says the same thing, then the gems are probably in your stomachs. Tomorrow morning, I will cut open your stomachs for the gems."

He ordered them to be put in a dark dungeon. All the travellers became worried at the words of the chief. They slept badly at night. The fourth traveller, who had planned to steal the gems, thought, 'When the chief is going to cut open their stomachs and find gems, then he will cut mine too.

So, my death is certain. Therefore, it is best to offer my stomach first and save the same people I had planned to kill in the first place. For when my stomach is cut open, the greedy chief will find nothing there. So, he will not suspect the others of having gems, and perhaps free them. Thus, by saving them, I will be doing a noble deed.'

So, he decided to carry out his plan. He did not reveal his plan to his three fellow companions.

Next morning, the four prisoners were taken to the village chief. The village chief gave them one last chance to own up about having the gems with them. "Tell me," he said, "where are the gems which the bird sings of?" The four travellers refused to answer his question. The chief became angry and ordered that each of their stomachs be cut open immediately. As the chief's men were preparing to cut open their stomachs, the thief begged the chief to cut open his stomach first. He added, "I cannot bear the sight of my brothers dying."

The chief agreed to his request. He found no gems in his stomach. Now, the chief was filled with repentance.

He said, "The bird's song filled me with greed. I have done a horrible deed. I am sure that these boys have no gems in their possession."

The three friends were freed and soon left the forest for safety. That is why, it is always said that it is better to have a sensible enemy than a foolish friend.

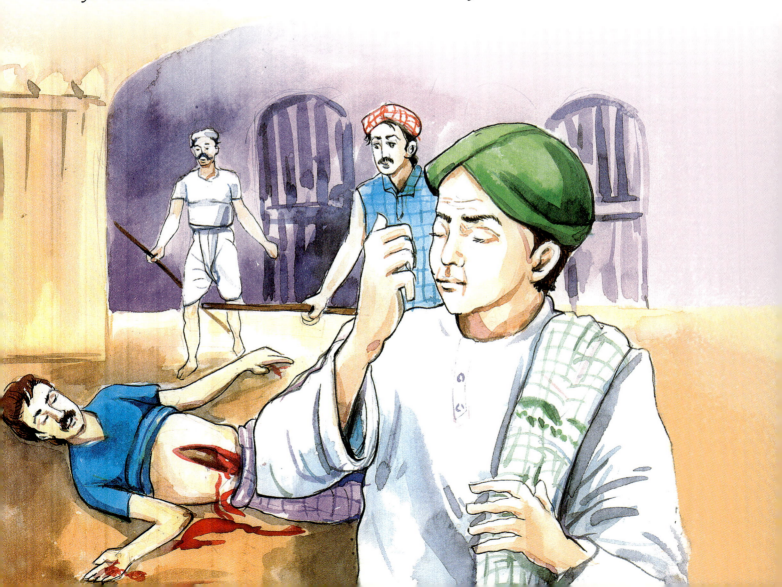

The Four Treasure-Seekers

Once upon a time, there lived four poor brahmins, who were the best of friends. The four friends were very ambitious and optimistic. They decided to earn some money. After thinking for a while, they decided to travel and trade. So, they bid farewell to their families and friends, and started on their journey.

Soon they came to a city, where they met a magician. They told him that they were travelling in order to earn a lot of money. The magician decided to help them. He prepared four magic quills and gave one to each brahmin.

He said, "Go to the northern slope of the Himalayas and wherever the quill drops,

the owner will surely find a great treasure there."

So, the brahmins set off for the Himalayas. The leader's quill fell first. After digging for some time, they found some copper coins. The leader took the coins and wanted to go back.

But the others said, "Fool! Copper coins will not make us rich. Leave it and let us all go further."

The leader of the brahmins disagreed with them and turned back with his copper coins.

The rest carried on with their journey. A little further away, another quill fell. When they dug, they found some silver coins.

The brahmin whose quill had fallen, wanted to take the coins and then turn back home.

The other two firmly believed that after copper and silver, they would find gold. So, they wished to go further. However, this brahmin decided not to accompany the other two and instead returned home.

The remaining two brahmins continued their journey. Then one of them dropped his quill.

They started digging and soon, they found gold. The owner was delighted. He suggested they return with the gold.

But his friend was convinced that his quill would lead to gems. His companion decided to wait for him while he continued with his journey in search of gems.

So, leaving his companion behind, the last brahmin travelled alone. The scorching heat made him very thirsty and so he started to search for water.

Then, he saw a man with blood dripping all over his body because a wheel was whirling on his head.

He immediately went to the man and asked him, "Why do you stand here with a rotating wheel on your head?"

The moment the brahmin spoke, the wheel left the man's head and settled on the brahmin's head.

"What happened?" asked the brahmin. "When will it go away? It hurts terribly."

"When a greedy person with a magic quill would come along and ask the same question, only then would the wheel lift from your head and settle on the other man's head," was the answer he got. The brahmin got scared.

The brahmin then asked the man, how long he had been standing there and what he had eaten all this while.

The man had suffered this torture for centuries. The god of wealth had prepared this terror to protect his wealth from greedy men and magicians. In the event that anyone came too close to his treasure, he was freed from hunger and thirst, only to bear this torture. Then the man left after answering the brahmin's questions. The brahmin was filled with deep anguish.

Meanwhile, the brahmin's companion, who was waiting for him to return, wondered why his friend was delayed.

So, he decided to follow his footprints. After a short while, he came across a man whose body was drenched in blood and who had a wheel whirling on his head. When he went nearer, he saw that the man was none other than his own dear friend. The brahmin's companion was shocked at the present state of his friend. Gradually, he recovered his voice.

"My friend, what happened?" he asked him.

The fourth brahmin told him the entire story. When his friend heard it, he scolded his friend saying, "Your greed has brought such misery on you. Now, you will have to suffer this punishment because of your greed."

Saying this, he turned around and went back home, leaving the brahmin to his fate.

How the Turtle Saved His Own Life

Once, there lived a king who had two young sons. To amuse them, he built a small lake in the courtyard. All day long, the two young princes played in the lake.

One day, the king ordered some fish to be put in the lake. Excited, the boys ran to see them. Besides the fish, there was a turtle too. They were happy to see the fish but had never seen a turtle before.

When the boys saw the turtle, they ran back to their father, crying, "There is a demon in the lake."

The turtle was brought to the palace. The princes were frightened once again. So, the king ordered it to be killed.

"How do we kill it?" asked one man.

"Pound it till it is crushed," said another man. Then an old man said, "Throw it into the lake, near the rocks. Then, it will die."

Then, the turtle said, "Why are you so cruel? I have never hurt you. Don't throw me into the water!" At this, the king ordered that the turtle be thrown into the lake.

The turtle laughed as he went back to his home. 'These foolish people don't realise just how safe I am here,' he thought, as he entered the river waters once again.

The Ox Who Won the Forfeit

Once, a man had a very strong ox. He went to a nearby village and announced, "I will pay you all a thousand silver coins if my ox does not draw a hundred wagons."

The villagers laughed at him and said, "Bring your ox. We will see if it succeeds."

The next day, the man brought his ox along. A huge crowd had gathered there.

The ox was then tied to the wagons.

Then, the owner beat his ox and said, "Move you rascal. Hurry up." The ox felt hurt and refused to move from the spot.

So, he was forced to pay and went home sadly. Once home, he sobbed, "My ox has carried the heaviest loads. Why did it he humiliate me?"

The next day, when he went to feed his ox, it said, "Why did you call me harsh names and beat me badly?"

The man realised his mistake and apologised to the ox.

"Tomorrow, I will draw the hundred carts and get back what you lost," said the ox. The next day, they went to the village. "I will pay double the silver if my ox does not pull a hundred carts," he declared to the people.

The ox dragged the load successfully. The villagers paid back the man all the money and said, "This ox is surely the strongest!"

The man and his ox returned home happily.

Why the Owl Is Not King of Birds

In ancient times, groups of people who lived together chose a king for themselves. The four-legged animals too chose a king. The fish in the sea chose a ruler and so the birds too decided to choose a king, saying, "Men, animals, and fish have kings, but we birds have no king. We ought to have one too. We must choose one soon."

All the birds agreed and decided to meet to discuss who their ruler should be.

So, the birds discussed among themselves as to who should be named as the king of birds. At last, they said, "Let us make the owl our new king."

At this, the old crow leapt up, saying, "No, I don't wish to see the owl as king. You all want him as king but he looks so cross right now.

If this is how he looks when he is happy, imagine how he would look when he is angry? I don't want an angry-looking king."

Thus, the crow disagreed and flew off. Since then, the crow and the owl have been bitter enemies.

Then, the turtle dove was chosen as the king of birds.

The White Elephant

Once, there lived a white king elephant who loved his mother dearly.

Every day, he searched for fruits for his ailing, blind mother. But she would never get any as his messengers would eat them instead. He was annoyed as she would go hungry and so they decided to leave. They arrived near a lake, filled with beautiful pink lotuses.

One day, he heard the screams of a man. They were of a forester, who had lost his way. When he saw the elephant, he became terrified but the elephant comforted him and led him to the fringe of the forest.

When the man reached his city, he heard that the king needed another elephant and it was announced that any man who had seen or heard of a valuable elephant should inform the king. Excited, he went to the king and told him about the white elephant.

The king sent his soldiers. The white elephant saw the king's men coming with the forester. He was hurt by the forester's ingratitude. But he quietly went, as he did not want to hurt anyone.

When the elephant did not return that night, his mother became worried. She had heard the noise outside and knew that the king's men had taken him away. She was terrified for her son.

When the white elephant entered the city, he found it beautifully decorated. A feast had been prepared for him, but the elephant would not eat. The king went to the stables. He wished to know why the elephant was unhappy.

The elephant said he missed his mother who was in the forest alone and sick. The king was filled with compassion and he set the white elephant free.

The elephant returned to the forest. He went to his mother and was relieved to see that she was well. He filled his trunk with water and sprayed it on his mother, who woke up and cried out for her son. The elephant affectionately stroked her and she immediately realised that it was her son. He told her that the king had released him. He promised her he would always look after her and never go away.

The Banyan Deer

In the forest, there lived two herds of deer with their kings — King Banyan Deer and King Branch Deer.

The king of the region enjoyed hunting and forced his subjects to join him. So, his subjects decided that they should capture the herds of deer and put them in the royal park for the king to hunt. On hearing this, the king was overjoyed. When he saw the two golden deer, he ordered that they were not to be killed.

Every day, the king's men would shoot arrows at the deer. Many would get hurt.

Then, one day, both the deer kings came up with a plan to stop the killing. They decided that each day, they would send a deer to the palace for slaughter.

One day, it was the turn of a female deer. She pleaded with King Banyan Deer, saying that her fawn was too young. He was filled with compassion. He promised her that he would send another deer in her place.

King Banyan Deer himself went to the palace. The king asked him why he was there. The deer narrated the story of the fawn and the doe. The king was greatly impressed by the concern the deer had and he spared him. But King Banyan Deer was not satisfied. He requested the king to spare all the deer. The king agreed.

King Banyan Deer was grateful and happy.

The Monkeys and the Water-Giant

Long ago, in a forest by a lake, there lived a giant who ate anyone who dared to enter its water.

In those days, a Bodhisattva had come down to the earth as the king of the monkeys. He commanded a troop of eighty thousand monkeys.

Once, he said to his followers, "My friends, this forest is not safe anymore. There are many fruits which are poisonous and also lakes that are haunted by water-giants. We have to be very careful about what we eat and drink.

"So, ask me before you eat any fruit which you have not eaten before or drink any water which you have not tasted before."

All the monkeys greatly valued their leader's advice and opinion and so they readily agreed to his suggestion.

One day, as the monkeys were wandering in the forest, they started to feel very thirsty. They came across a lake. They were not aware of the fact that the water-giant lived there. Remembering their leader's advice, they decided not to drink the water and waited for him.

When he came, the thirsty monkeys asked if they could drink water from the lake. The leader looked carefully at the footprints around and saw that they led to the lake but none came out.

He thought for a while and realised that a water-giant must be hiding in the lake. He said, "My brothers, I am certain that this lake is haunted. I suggest that we do not drink this water."

The water-giant had been listening to their conversation very intently. Suddenly, he emerged from the centre of the lake. With his blue belly, white face, and red hands and feet, he was quite a horrible sight.

All the monkeys were frightened when they saw this dreadful creature.

He shouted to the monkeys, "What are you waiting for? Why don't you drink the water?"

The leader asked him, "Are you the water-giant who eats up all the animals entering the lake?"

"Yes I am, and I will eat all of you too," he said.

"We will drink water from this lake, but we will not let you eat us," said the monkeys.

"And how are you going to do that?" said the creature.

Suddenly, all the monkeys became quiet. They looked at their leader to help them.

"Simple, we will drink the water without entering the lake!" replied the leader.

He asked a monkey from his troop to bring him a reed. He chanted some mantras (sacred verses) and at once, the reed became hollow.

Then he went around the lake and said, "May all the reeds growing around this lake become hollow." And all the reeds became hollow.

After this, the leader and the eighty thousand monkeys seated themselves around the lake, each with a reed in his hands.

Then, the leader sucked water through the reed and all the others followed.

The water-giant was so shocked that he didn't know what to do. He swam to the edge of the lake, trying to get hold of at least one of the eighty thousand monkeys, but all in vain.

The monkeys drank water to their heart's content and quenched their thirst without going into the lake.

The water-giant could not eat them. Hungry and enraged, he returned home to the bottom of the lake.

All the monkeys thanked the wise leader and praised him for his wit and intelligence.

The Wise Goat and the Jackal

Once, on the slopes of the Himalayas, there lived hundreds of goats. Not far from there, a jackal called Putimamsa lived with his wife Veni.

One day, as they were wandering in search of food, Putimamsa saw a herd of goats and wanted to eat them.

A few days later, he was able to kill a goat and he and his wife had a feast. Gradually, he killed all the goats except one called Melamata. In spite of all his tricks, he could never kill Melamata. Then, he thought of a plan.

He told his wife to befriend the goat. "When you have become friends, I will lie down and pretend to be dead. Then you must say to the goat, 'My husband is dead and I am all alone. Please help me bury his body.' And when she comes with you, I will kill her," said the jackal. The wife agreed.

Gradually, Veni and Melamata became friends. Soon she gained the confidence of the goat and informed her husband.

So the next day, Putimamsa pretended to be dead. The wife asked the goat to help her bury him. However, the goat refused saying, "Your husband has killed all my relatives. I am scared of him. I will not come with you."

"How can the dead harm you?" asked the jackal's wife. She begged the goat to come with her.

The goat thought for some time and finally agreed to go with her.

But on the way, she had second thoughts. To be on the safe side, she made her friend walk ahead of her, while she kept a close watch on the jackal.

When the jackal heard the footsteps, he raised his head and, rolling his eyes, looked around.

As Veni and the goat reached Putimamsa, he got up, ready to kill the goat. Seeing this, the goat realised she had been tricked and ran away to save her life.

Unhappy, the jackal thought of another plan. He asked his wife to try again.

So Veni went to the goat and said, "My friend, I am grateful to you. You appeared and my lord regained consciousness! He wants to thank you. Please come with me."

The goat thought, 'The wretch wants to kill me. I must also deceive her.'

She agreed but said that a hundred dogs would accompany her, and if they didn't find food, they would kill both the jackals.

When the jackal heard this, she got scared and fled, never to return.

The Robbers and the Treasure

Once upon a time, there was a brahmin who knew the special Vaidarbha charm. When the planets were at a particular conjunction, the chanting of this charm would lead to a shower of gems from the sky. At that time, a Bodhisattva became the brahmin's pupil.

One day, the two were passing through a forest. A gang of thieves caught them. The brahmin begged the thieves to let them go but the robbers didn't listen. They sent the pupil home to get money. Promising to return soon, the pupil warned his master not to chant the charm or both the brahmin and the robbers would suffer.

The robbers tied the brahmin to a nearby tree. The hour of the great conjunction was near.

'Why should I suffer this misery? With the charm, I can bring about the shower of gems. The robbers can take all the gems and let me go,' he thought.

So, he told the robbers about the charm and what it could do. The robbers were very interested. The brahmin asked them to untie him so that he could have a bath and perform puja (an act of worship). Only then, would there be a shower of gems.

The robbers suspected that he was lying, but their greed overpowered all. The brahmin convinced them that he really knew the Vaidarbha charm. So, the robbers untied him.

At the moment of the planetary conjunction, the brahmin chanted the charm. Soon, a shower of gems came down from the sky, which the robbers quickly gathered. Another gang of robbers had seen this. They came and seized the first group and grabbed the treasure.

"If you want the treasure, catch the brahmin who, by simply looking at the sky, has brought down the gems," said the robbers of the first gang.

So the second gang released the first gang and caught the brahmin instead. "Shower down gems for us too," they demanded.

"It would give me great pleasure to give you what you want, but it will be a year before the particular conjunction of planets takes place again. You will have to wait for another year," said the brahmin, scared.

The robbers got very angry and killed the brahmin. They then hurried after the first gang of robbers, killed them and took the loot.

When the pupil returned, all he saw was dead corpses. Then, he saw the dead body of his teacher.

"I had warned him not to chant the charm. But he did not listen to me. As a result, he has brought death upon himself and the others," said the pupil.

He cremated his teacher's body and left.

The Hypocritical Jackal

Once upon a time, a Bodhisattva was born as a very wise rat. He lived in the forest with hundreds of other rats. He was as huge as a young boar. All the other rats had great regard for him.

In the same forest there lived a cunning jackal, who had an eye on these rats. He had, for a long time, wanted to eat these rats. So he thought of a clever plan to catch and eat them.

He went near their dwelling and facing the sun, he stood on one leg. He continued this for many days.

One day, when the Bodhisattva went out in search of food, he saw the jackal in this unusual pose.

He observed the jackal closely and thought that he was a saintly being who was engrossed in his meditation. So, he decided to talk to him.

"What is your name my friend?" asked the Bodhisattva.

"Godly is my name," said the jackal.

'Such a holy name,' thought the rat.

Then out of curiosity, he asked the jackal, "O divine one, why are you standing on one leg?"

The jackal had already prepared the answer to this question. It was all part of his plan. "I stand on one leg to help mother earth. If I stand on all four legs, the earth will not be able to bear my weight," replied the sly jackal.

On hearing this, the Bodhisattva was very pleased.

The rat's curiosity about the jackal grew. "Why do you keep your mouth open?" he asked.

"To breathe in the fresh air. I live on air. That is my only food," said the jackal.

Amazed with the jackal's answers, the rat further went on and asked, "Why do you face the sun?"

"I worship the sun," said the jackal.

The Bodhisattva was highly impressed with the jackal. He told the other rats about the jackal.

Every morning, the Bodhisattva and the other rats came to pay their respects to the jackal.

The jackal was very happy because now that he had gained their trust, he could put his plan into action.

Every day when the rats would be on their way home, after paying their respects to the jackal, he would grab the last rat and eat it. So nobody even realised that the jackal had eaten one of the rats.

With every passing day, the rats became fewer and fewer in number. All the rats started getting worried. They went to the Bodhisattva and shared their concern. The Bodhisattva too had noticed the decrease in the rat population. He suspected the jackal and decided to test him.

So the next day, after paying their respects to the jackal, the Bodhisattva decided to let the other rats go first. He followed them at the end of the group.

As usual, the jackal tried to grab the last rat to eat it, but the Bodhisattva was too quick for him.

He turned around and shouted at him, "You are actually a devil in the garb of a saint. You pretend to be very pious, but you are very cunning!"

The jackal was taken aback by what had just happened. He did not know how to react and so he pounced on the Bodhisattva again. The Bodhisattva started screaming and shouting.

Hearing the commotion, all the rats realised what must have happened. They all turned back immediately and started to run towards the jackal and the Bodhisattva.

All the rats rose up against the jackal and attacked him. They made sure that the wicked jackal was killed and would never trouble any animal again.

And thus, the Bodhisattva, with his friends killed the evil jackal who had tricked them.

The Woodpecker, the Tortoise and the Antelope

Once upon a time, a Bodhisattva was born as an antelope. He lived in a beautiful forest near a lake. In the same lake lived a tortoise, and not very far away from there lived a woodpecker on a tree. The three were very good friends. They always helped each other.

One day, there was a hunter roaming around the forest. He saw an animal's footprints leading to the lake. 'These look like an antelope's footprints. It must be living somewhere near the lake. I shall hunt it down,' he thought.

He quickly ran to his hut and got a net, large enough to hold an antelope.

"The antelope will definitely come to the lake to drink water," he said aloud. So he set the trap for the antelope. Then he searched for a hiding place for himself. He decided to hide behind a large tree, from where he could keep a watch over the trap he had set. Knowing that it would be a long wait, the hunter hid behind the tree and waited patiently for the antelope to return.

That night, the antelope came to the lake to drink water. Unaware of the trap that had been set, the antelope got caught in it.

He tried to escape but was unable to move. Seeing that the antelope had been caught, the hunter emerged from behind the tree.

In distress, the antelope started shouting for help. The tortoise and the woodpecker heard their friend's cries and decided to help him.

The woodpecker said to the tortoise, "We have to save our friend. You tear the net with your teeth. Meanwhile, I will keep the hunter busy so that he does not come near the lake. If we are successful, then our friend can escape and will not die."

So the tortoise began to gnaw at the trap and the woodpecker stood guard over the hunter's hut. He waited patiently all night. In the morning, when the hunter came out of his hut, the woodpecker struck him hard on his face.

The hunter cried out in pain. 'Some bird of ill omen has struck me,' he thought and rushed back into the hut. He waited for some time till the pain subsided. Then he decided to go out again but this time through the back door.

The woodpecker thought, 'He came out through the front door last time. He might use the back door now.' So he went to the back door and waited for the hunter. When the hunter came out, the woodpecker struck again.

"Oh! This bird is not going to let me go for work today. I think I'll stay indoors and go tomorrow," said the hunter.

On hearing this, the woodpecker felt relieved. 'I am sure that tortoise will be able to set antelope free by tomorrow morning,' he thought to himself.

The next morning, seeing the hunter come out of his hut, the woodpecker quickly flew back to his friends to warn them.

The tortoise had managed to tear the net by this time. When the antelope saw the hunter, he ran away, but the tortoise wasn't able to run because he had become weak from all the hard work. The hunter caught him, put him in a bag, and started for home.

The antelope was determined to save his friend. So, he lay down in the hunter's path, pretending to be weak.

Seeing the antelope, the hunter dropped the tortoise and tried to catch him. But the antelope got up and ran. He led the hunter deep into the forest. When he was sure that the hunter could not catch him, he slipped away.

He then returned to the spot where the tortoise was tied in the bag. He ripped the bag open and freed the tortoise.

Then he told his friends to hide because the hunter was sure to come back.

The woodpecker flew away, the tortoise hid in the water and the antelope hid among the trees. The hunter came back but did not see them and went home, unhappy.

Thereafter, the three friends lived happily with each other.

The Flight of the Beasts

Once upon a time, a Bodhisattva was born as a young lion. He lived in a dense forest with several other animals. All the animals respected him a lot.

One day, a hare was sitting under a bael tree. He was thinking about the end of the earth. He thought, 'If the earth breaks open suddenly, what will happen to me?' At that very moment, a ripe bael fruit fell on the ground and rolled over some dry leaves.

The hare jumped up. He could not understand what had made that sound. He looked around but could not see anything and so he sat down under the tree again.

Suddenly, another bael fruit fell on the ground. Now, the hare panicked.

The hare thought that the sound of the falling fruit was actually the earth splitting. 'Oh dear! The earth is actually falling apart. I should run to save my life,' he thought. He got up and started running away from the bael tree.

Another hare saw him running. He asked the first hare, "Brother, what happened? Why are you running?"

"The earth is breaking open! I saw it myself," cried the first hare. This scared the second hare and he also started running along with the first hare.

One by one, they were seen by a deer, a goat, a buffalo, a jackal, a tiger, a zebra, an elephant and many other animals of the jungle.

On asking the hares why they were running, all the animals were told that the earth was cracking. So, all the other animals also started running with the hares.

The lion saw the herd of animals. He asked them, "Why are you all running?" All the animals replied in unison, "The earth is breaking. We are running to save our lives." "You should also come with us," added the goat and all the animals started running again.

But the lion did not believe them. He thought, 'The earth cannot split. They must have heard some other noise which they have mistaken for the splitting of the earth. I have to stop them or their ignorance will kill them all. I will have to save their lives.'

He roared as loud as he could and all the animals got scared and stopped in their tracks.

Then the lion asked them, "Who saw the earth cracking?"

"The elephant saw it," one of them said.

So the lion asked the elephant, "Is it true? Did you see the earth splitting?"

The elephant shook his head and said, "I did not see it myself, but the tiger told me."

The tiger said, "The deer told me."

The deer said, "The buffalo told me."

The buffalo said, "The giraffe told me."

The giraffe said, "The zebra told me."

The zebra said, "The goat told me."

This went on till it came to the first hare who had actually heard the noise.

The lion asked the hare, "Did you actually see the earth cracking?"

"Yes, I saw the earth splitting," replied the hare.

"Where did you see this?" asked the lion curiously.

The hare told him about the noise he had heard twice near the bael tree. "The first time I didn't get scared, but when the noise recurred, I realised that the earth was breaking," said the hare.

The lion thought, 'A ripe bael fruit must have fallen and this must have frightened the hare. I will have to find out the truth.'

He asked the hare to show him the spot and instructed the rest of the animals to stay there till his return.

The hare took the lion to the spot. The lion went to the foot of the bael tree. Lying nearby was the ripe bael fruit.

'So I was right,' thought the lion and went back to the herd of animals.

He told them the whole story and asked them not to worry. Reassured, the animals returned to their dwellings. Thus, the lion's presence of mind saved the lives of all the animals.

The Pigeon and the Crow

During Brahmadatta's reign in Benaras, a Bodhisattva was born as a pigeon.

It was a common practice then to hang straw baskets in the homes, to provide shelter and comfort to birds.

There lived a rich goldsmith in Benaras. His cook had hung one such basket in his kitchen. A pigeon, who was the Bodhisattva, came to stay there.

This pigeon would not eat anything from the kitchen. It would go out daily in search of food and return in the evening. Even if he did not find any food, he would stay hungry, but he would never steal from the goldsmith's kitchen.

One day, a crow was flying outside the goldsmith's kitchen. He smelled fish and meat being cooked and his mouth started watering.

After spending the whole day wondering how to enter the kitchen, in the evening, when he saw the pigeon going into the kitchen to rest in the straw basket, he got an idea.

Early next morning, he followed the pigeon, when he went out in search of food. The pigeon saw the crow following him and asked, "Why are you following me, my friend?"

The crow was prepared to answer this question. Bowing his head a little, he started speaking.

"My Lord," said the crow, "I am very impressed by the way you conduct yourself. I want to learn from you. Therefore, I wish to come with you."

"Thank you for your kind words but I have come out to search for food, and my kind of food is quite different from yours," said the pigeon.

"Oh, that doesn't matter. When you search for your food, I will search for mine," said the crow.

The pigeon reluctantly agreed. So, while the pigeon searched for seeds, the crow ate insects.

In the evening, the pigeon flew back to the goldsmith's kitchen and the crow went with him.

The cook was surprised to see another bird in his kitchen. He hung up another straw basket for the crow. The crow was very glad that his plan had succeeded.

Thereafter, the crow and the pigeon lived together in the kitchen. They went out every morning to search for their food and returned in the evening.

One day, the cook hung up a fish in the kitchen. The crow wanted to eat it. So, he thought of a plan to stay at home the next day.

He spent the whole night groaning. Next day, when the pigeon was about to leave, he called out to the crow, "Come, my friend, let's go."

"I cannot come with you today. I have a stomach ache," replied the crow.

The pigeon was surprised because he had never heard of a crow with a stomach ache. He realised that he must be after the fish. He told the crow, "I know that you want to eat this fish, but it is the goldsmith's food. I don't approve of your greed. So give it up and come with me."

But the crow refused to listen. Before flying away to search for food, the pigeon again warned the crow, saying, "This greed of yours will do you no good. The goldsmith has provided us with shelter in his house. We should not steal from him."

But the greedy crow did not pay any attention to the pigeon's advice.

Meanwhile, the cook put the fish into the cooking pot and went outside. 'The cook has gone out. This is my chance to quickly eat the fish and fly away,' thought the crow.

He tried to remove the lid of the pot, but it fell on the ground, with a thud so loud that it could be heard all through the house.

The cook heard the noise and came running inside. He saw the lid of the cooking pot on the floor and the crow near the pot. "You wicked crow! My master provided you with shelter in his house and this is how you repay him. You should be taught a lesson," said the cook, angrily.

He caught hold of the crow and plucked every feather off his body. The crow began to wince in pain. He then ground some ginger, salt and cumin, mixed it with buttermilk and put the crow in it. He then put the crow back in the basket.

When the pigeon came back in the evening, he saw the crow groaning in pain. He went and sat next to him.

"I warned you not to be greedy," said the pigeon. "But you would not listen to me. Your greed is responsible for your pain. I cannot live here anymore." Saying this, the pigeon flew away.

Soon after, the crow died and the cook threw him into the dustbin.

The Musicians

Once, there lived a father and son who were very talented musicians. They used to play the drums at wedding ceremonies. They worked very hard to earn their living.

One day, it so happened that they were invited to perform at a music festival in Benaras. Both father and son were very excited and decided to participate in the festival.

People from all parts of the country had come to attend the music festival. The audience enjoyed their show so much that by the end of the festival, they had collected plenty of gifts. Some people gave them money, some gave them beautiful clothes, and some even presented them with jewels!

After the festival had ended, the father and son were very happy. The money they had collected would last them for quite a few months. They both slept very peacefully that night and decided to start the long journey back to their village, early next morning.

On the way back, they had to cross a dense forest. As they were passing through the forest, the son started beating the drum.

"Son, what are you doing? Don't beat the drums. The robbers will hear the noise and catch us," said the father.

"Don't worry, Father. I will play a martial beat to scare them away," said the son, as he continued beating the drums.

"Son, I am warning you. This forest is not safe. We will get into trouble," said the father. But the son just wouldn't listen.

Some thieves, who were hiding in the forest, heard the beating of the drums.
"I think a royal party is hunting in the forest," said one of them.

Thongh the martial beat is played only once, the son played it continuously. He did not stop, despite his father's persistent warnings.

The robbers became suspicious when they heard the continuous beating of drums. They realised it was somebody who might have earned a lot of money and was feeling happy. So, they tracked down the father and the son and attacked them. Taking all their money and jewels, they ran away.

"I told you to stop but you would not listen to me. Due to your foolish pride, you have invited your own bad fortune by playing at the wrong time," scolded the father.

"I am sorry, Father. I have learnt my lesson now," said the son.

The Donkey in the Lion's Skin

Once upon a time, in a village, lived a cunning merchant. He used to go from place to place to sell his goods. The goods were carried by a donkey.

Whenever the donkey felt hungry, the merchant would remove the goods, put a lion's skin over its back and let it loose in the fields. If the farmers saw the animal in their fields, they took it to be a lion and did not dare to enter the fields to drive it away.

This went on successfully for quite a few years. No matter which village they were in, the merchant would put the lion skin over the donkey and he would go eat his fill in the fields, without anyone coming near him.

One day, the merchant stopped at a village. Sitting down to eat himself, he let the donkey also loose in a barley field with the lion's skin over it.

A farmer was walking by the field. He spotted the donkey and mistaking it for a lion, he hurried towards the village and informed the villagers about the lion there.

The frightened villagers decided to do something. So, they thought of a plan. "Let's scare it out of the field and then catch it," said one villager. "Where will we get such a big net to catch it? Let's just kill it," said another. "Yes, yes," they all shouted.

They went to the field with their sticks. When they reached the field, they started beating the drums. The donkey got very scared and started braying.

The villagers, on hearing the donkey bray, realised that it was not a lion. They beat it till it was nearly dead.

A few hours later, when the donkey did not return, the merchant became a little worried. 'The donkey usually returns soon. I wonder why my donkey has not come back as yet,' he thought.

The merchant decided to go and look for his animal. While he was searching for his donkey, he saw it lying on the ground, half-dead. The merchant felt sorry for the wounded animal.

He asked a farmer what had happened. After the farmer had narrated the whole story to the merchant, he thought that had the donkey not brayed, it would not have been beaten up so badly. The donkey died soon after and the merchant left the place, filled with sorrow and remorse.